W9-CQB-036

DATE DUE

BAECHTEL GROVE SCHOOL
1150 MAGNOLIA STREET
WILLITS, CALIFORNIA

ELEPHANT SEALS

ELEPHANT SEALS

Louise C. Brown

*Illustrated with photographs by Andrée Abecassis
and drawings by Nina Inez Brown*

DODD, MEAD & COMPANY
NEW YORK

ACKNOWLEDGMENTS

The author wishes to acknowledge the invaluable assistance of The Center for Coastal Marine Studies, University of California, Santa Cruz; the California State Park System, San Mateo Coast Area; Donald Strainey, University of California's Museum of Vertebrate Zoology, Berkeley; and Joan Cohn, Oakland Public Schools.

Library of Congress Cataloging in Publication Data

Brown, Louise C
  Elephant seals.

  Includes index.
  SUMMARY: Presents a brief look at the life cycle of elephant seals and their remarkable comeback from near extinction.
  1. Elephant seals—Juvenile literature. [1. Elephant seals. 2. Seals (Animals)] I. Abecassis, Andrée. II. Brown, Nina Inez. III. Title.
QL737.P64B74   599'.748   78-25623
ISBN 0-396-07665-3

*To Audrey for introducing me to
these remarkable sea mammals*

A close-up look at the snout, whiskers, and scarred neck of a male elephant seal.

What a strange-looking animal the male elephant seal is. Some people think he must be one of Nature's mistakes. Others say he's a wonder, a mighty marvel of the sea.

Look at him! Have you ever seen such a mountain of fat? He has so much blubber, his skin shakes and shivers when he shuffles over the sandy beach. He is as heavy as a hippopotamus and as shapeless as a stuffed sausage. With his rough fur coat, his wrinkled neck covered with scars, and a nose so long it flops down over his mouth, he is not very handsome.

Watch him as he comes out of the ocean and onto land. His foreflippers stretch forward like two stubby arms and his shoulder muscles bulge. His rubbery spine bends upward, his hindflippers give a sudden push. WHOOSH! His whole body jerks along like a huge caterpillar. Every movement on land seems to be an effort. Hitching and heaving his body over the sand, he slowly crawls to a spot he likes.

But don't let his slowness fool you. When he wants to, he can move as fast as you can run. If you stood too close, he could lift his big hindflippers up in the air and knock you flat with one powerful swat.

There isn't much chance that this would ever happen. You're not likely to bump into an elephant seal while walking on the beach. As a matter of fact, not many people have seen one. They are unusual animals and are found only in a few isolated parts of the world.

The elephant seal wasn't always a rare sight. During the last century, about 150 years ago, there were hundreds of thousands of them roaming the seas.

There are two species of elephant seals. There is the northern elephant seal (*Mirounga angustirostris*) that lives in the Pacific Ocean along the coast of California and Mexico. And there is a larger cousin, the southern elephant seal (*Mirounga leonina*) that inhabits the icy cold waters of Antarctica. Today, their herds are greatly reduced.

A passerby quickly sidesteps the dangerous hindflippers.

It is easy to see how the elephant seal earned his name. The first to discover this animal were sailors who thought the male looked like an elephant because of his huge size and his long nose. But for all that, he is really a seal—a pinniped. (Pinnipedia is a scientific suborder which includes seals and walruses. This group of animals has flippers—*pinna*—instead of feet—*pedia*.)

Like all other seals, the elephant seal is a warm-blooded mammal that breathes air and can stay on land for extended periods of time. And, like other mammals, the newborn pups are nourished with milk from their mothers.

Although the northern and southern elephant seals have similar habits, much more is known about the northern species because of recent studies made by scientists in California.

The male northern elephant seal is gigantic. Often fifteen feet long and four feet thick across the middle, he is a solid mass of bone, blubber, and muscle. When full

Opposite: *At first glance, the male elephant seal could be mistaken for an elephant.*

The size of the male elephant seal is gargantuan in comparison to his mate.

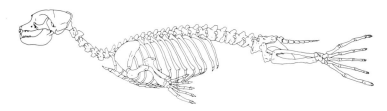

Drawing of the skeleton of a northern elephant seal.

grown, one of these bulls can weigh as much as four thousand pounds. Some really large ones are six thousand pounds. That's two to three tons!

The female, on the other hand, seems small next to her mate. From the tip of her nose to the end of her hind-flippers, she is only about half as long and seldom more than fifteen hundred pounds. And her nose is different. It is much, much shorter than his.

Look at the drawing of the skeleton. See the five sets of finger bones? It is true that these fingers have grown together into a flipper that helps the elephant seal swim faster in the water. But the elephant seal can still use its fingers to scratch its nose or clean its fur. More than that, it can scoop up a handful of sand and throw it

Even the hindflippers can be helpful when it comes to scratching an itchy "foot."

with deadly aim at a target. Whenever any insects or bothersome sea gulls irritate an elephant seal, it will flip a stream of sand straight at the pests. And it seldom misses.

This ability to flip sand also serves another purpose. It's the way an elephant seal can keep cool while lying on the beach. With a few flip-flip-flips it can quickly cover its back with sand and be protected from the sun's hot rays.

A female flipping sand on her back to hit annoying insects.

On land, the elephant seal uses its strong hindflippers to get from one spot to another. In the ocean, these powerful flippers help it shoot through the water like a streamlined rocket. Down, down, down it goes. Down to the bottom for its favorite foods—squid and dogfish and skate and ratfish.

Scientists aren't sure how deep elephant seals can dive, but they do know that they can go at least five hundred feet below the surface because that's where ratfish often live. That is almost a tenth of a mile—as far as from the rooftop of a fifty-story building down to the sidewalk.

That far down, the sea is bitter cold and very dark. At that depth, the water pressure could crush most skeletons. Deep-sea divers who go down that far must wear metal suits to protect themselves. But the elephant seal has no trouble. It has a thick, six-inch layer of fat to keep it warm. And its eyes are curved in a special way so it can pick up the faint rays of light when hunting for food on the ocean

Opposite: *Elephant seals like to eat (from top to bottom) squid, skate, and ratfish.*

floor. But why its ribs aren't crushed, or why its lungs don't collapse, is still a mystery.

At sea, the elephant seal is a smooth, swift swimmer. If it wants, it can stop and float and even go fast asleep for awhile. Like many other sea mammals—the dolphins and whales and even manatees—the elephant seal is able to stay underwater for long periods of time. It must, for if it has to swim down a tenth of a mile to find its food, it has to swim another tenth of a mile before it can return to the surface for air.

Scientists are beginning to learn more and more about the habits of the northern elephant seal. They know it comes on land for a few months out of the year, first to breed and later to molt. But scientists don't really know where it spends the other eight or nine months when it's out at sea. Does it migrate thousands of miles like the gray whale? Does it go to the same feeding grounds? Does it swim alone, or does it stay with other elephant seals in large herds?

It is known that the elephant seal "hauls out" of the water twice a year. Once is during the winter, usually from

A bull crawling onto the beach after a quick dip.

December to the end of March, for the breeding season. This is the time when the pups are born. The elephant seal also comes on land in late spring or early summer. This is the time it molts—the time when large patches of its coarse fur coat fall out and the elephant seal has to wait for the new hair to grow in again.

During the first days in December, some instinct pulls the male elephant seal away from his feast of squid and ratfish, reminding him it is time to go ashore. Among the first to arrive on the beach is the Alpha bull. He is the bull that was the biggest and strongest of them all last year and the beachmaster of the herd. But if he wants to be in charge again, he will have to fight the other big bulls that come ashore.

As the weeks go by, other males begin to "haul out" on land. Soon, the beach is a noisy battleground with bulls chasing, clashing, challenging each other to see which is the strongest.

Snorting and roaring, the fighting bulls can be heard almost a mile away. What an odd sound! It's not like the throaty roar of a lion, or the trumpet screech of a charging

The roar of a bull elephant seal can be heard a great distance. It is sometimes used to serve as a warning to other males to keep away from his cows.

African elephant. It's not a hoot, or a honk, or a howl. It's unlike anything you've ever heard before. To tell the truth, the sound is so weird, it doesn't seem possible that it comes from a living animal.

First, the elephant seal bull fills his trunk with air until it blows up like a balloon and is twice its normal size. Then, opening his jaws and throwing his head back so his swollen nose hangs down to his mouth, he shoots three or four blasts of air through his throat. CLAACK! CLAACK! CLAACK! One after another, the sharp blasts explode against his air-filled trunk which seems to amplify the sound like a loudspeaker.

Some say the sound is like a snare drum, some say it's like the backfiring of a car. Others say it's like cannonballs hitting a wooden fence.

The bull's loud CLAACK is a warning that he is willing to challenge any other male that comes near. This is usually enough to scare the others away. But not always. And then the fight is ugly. And bloody. Lifting his chest and torso high off the ground, the elephant seal stands only inches away from his opponent, swaying from side to side

Male elephant seals challenge one another to a fight for control of the females of the herd. They often raise more than half their bodies off the ground.

and waiting for the right moment to attack. WHACK!
His strong jaws clamp down on the other fellow's neck
or chest like a steel trap. WHACK! This time his razor-
sharp teeth tear into the other one's trunk. WHACK!
WHACK! A few more bites and the fight is over.

The neck and throat are favorite targets during a fight.

There are times, however, when such fights are really serious. These can last as long as thirty to forty minutes.

The winner, often the biggest and certainly the strongest, then becomes the Alpha bull. He will have the right to mate with as many females, or cows, as he wishes. But he's not the only prizewinner in this contest of strength. Sometimes there is a prize waiting for those that tie for second place, usually three or four strong bulls that defeated all the other males except the Alpha bull himself. When the number of cows that come on shore are too many for one beachmaster to handle, he will allow these next-in-line bulls to mate with some of the younger females. All the other bulls—the old ones, the young ones, the defeated ones—will stay on the sidelines waiting for a chance to mate with some cows when the top bulls are off guard.

While the bulls are battling on the beaches for control of a harem, the females begin to appear offshore. They are anxious to land. It is time for their pups to be born.

Unlike the bulls, the cows are more sociable creatures

Though big, ungainly, and unattractive, the male can be tender with his cows.

that seem to enjoy huddling together. Side by side, sometimes resting their heads on each other's shoulders, they lie on the sand in tightly packed bunches. From a distance, they look like piles of driftwood.

About a week after she comes out of the water, the cow gives birth to a single, black, woolly pup. It may be anywhere from 65 to 110 pounds when it is born. Weak and whimpering much of the day, it nuzzles against its mother to feed on her rich, creamy milk. Her milk is so rich, the pup gains eight to ten pounds each day. In eleven days,

The young pups' whiskers, eyebrows, and fingernails are well formed at birth.

A newborn pup is as appealing as a puppy.

A pup nursing.

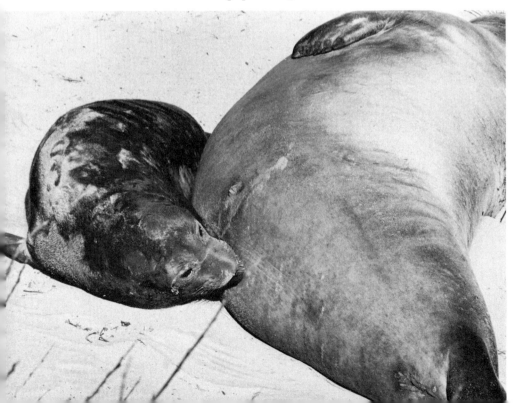

It doesn't take long for young pups to learn that their fingers are for scratching...

...or sucking.

In a few years, this youngster will be as big as the older male, Linus. Researchers sometimes identify individual seals by writing their names on them with Clorox.

the pup has often doubled its weight. When it is a month old, the pup weighs almost three hundred pounds!

This is the end of the nursing period. It is time for the cow to mate again.

Changing almost overnight from a passive mother that allowed her pup to nurse whenever it was hungry, she suddenly becomes its enemy. She does not want it near her anymore. If it tries to nurse, she will attack.

The pup is on its own. Now called a weaner because it has stopped nursing, it will find others its own age and

When a pup is abandoned by its mother, it sometimes has trouble finding another female willing to let him nurse.

A weaner argues with a younger pup.

settle in a safe spot on the beach. By this time, it will have lost its black fur coat and will have a shiny, gray-brown one instead. It will now discover—all by itself—how to swim, how to catch fish, and how to eat solid food. Here it will stay for a month or so until it is strong enough to swim in the deep ocean.

Right after mating, the cow disappears into the sea. She has been on land for almost six weeks. The bull, on the other hand, has been at the breeding station for three to four months. Most of this time, he has been out of the water, returning to the nearby surf only for short dips to cool himself. During all this time, he has eaten nothing at all. This may explain why he is so much bigger than the female; he needs this extra supply of fat to give him extra energy at this time. But scientists are still puzzled by his ability to survive for so long without eating. How can he be so active if he doesn't eat? How can he drag his two-ton body around on land without getting weak?

Even more surprising to scientists is the fact that the female doesn't seem to lose more weight after she has finished nursing her pup. She, too, doesn't eat anything during the five to six weeks she's on land. At the end of her stay on shore during the breeding season, her pup has managed to gain an extra two hundred pounds just from her milk. And yet she seems as fat and plump as she was when she first arrived.

When the last of the females have left the beach, the bulls also return to the open sea. Where they go, no one really knows. Some say they wander wherever there is food. Some think they travel along certain routes to the same spots each year.

Wherever they go, there is no doubt they return to land again in summer for the molting season to shed patches of their fur. How different the molting season is from the lively breeding months! At this time, the elephant seals are asleep most of the day and night. They rarely move.

Before long, the fur on the neck and throat begins to peel off, leaving patches of bare skin that are tender and sometimes painful. In fact, the skin is so tender it can get badly sunburned. There is not much the elephant seal can do about it except cover itself with sand or lie quietly in shallow water for a few weeks until the fur grows back.

Anyone who has ever seen a herd of molting elephant seals can tell you they're sleepy, harmless giants at this time of year. Only half-awake and unwilling to move because of their tender skin, they were easy targets for hunters.

It didn't take long for the men in the old whaling boats to realize this. Up until the eighteenth century, when whaling became an important industry and men were sailing all over the world to find a good catch, the elephant seal had almost no enemies. Sometimes, the young pups would be killed by a shark or a killer whale. But other than that, they were safe.

The elephant seal's natural enemy—the killer whale—a fierce sea mammal with razor-sharp teeth and powerful jaws. They are often seen swimming in packs with their black dorsal fins just above the waterline.

They were safe until the fateful day when a whaling ship came upon a herd of molting elephant seals, and the crew realized that these strange animals were valuable as a source of oil. Each one caught by the whalers provided at least eighty gallons of high quality oil. A full-grown bull sometimes furnished as much as two hundred gallons. More important, the elephant seals were easier to catch than whales. Hundreds could be killed at once.

Herd after herd was destroyed. By 1889, most of the northern elephant seals in the Pacific Ocean were gone. By the end of the century, people were sure they had all disappeared, that they were extinct.

Somehow, a handful survived. In 1911, a small herd of northern elephant seals was found on the Island of Guadalupe near the coast of Baja California. Only a dozen were still alive. To protect these few survivors, the Mexican government passed a law to stop the killing of elephant seals and even went so far as to station soldiers on the island to see that the law was enforced.

Since then, the northern elephant seal has made a remarkable, astonishing comeback from the days when there was just one tiny colony left on Guadalupe. Today, there are more than forty thousand! In fact, there are so many now, they have had to find breeding grounds on other small, unpopulated islands and beaches along the coast of Mexico and California—from the San Benito and Cedros islands off Baja California to the Año Nuevo and Farallon islands near San Francisco.

A herd of elephant seals on the beach.

There is still a great deal to be learned about this unusual sea mammal. Some scientists report that stones have been found in the elephant seal's stomach. Are the stones eaten to stop hunger pangs when it stays on land so long? Are the stones used like a scuba diver's weights to help it stay down when it is at the bottom of the sea? Just when does it eat the stones—when it is on land or in the ocean?

Scientists would like to know more about this strange creature of the sea. Someday they will. And when they do, they'll find more answers to the mystery of how life exists in the oceans of the world.

How would you like to meet this "monster" in the dark?

INDEX

(Page numbers in *italic* are those on which illustrations appear)

Alpha bull, 24, 29
Año Nuevo, 41
Antarctica, 13

Baja California, 40, 41
Birth of pups, 31
Blubber, 11, 20, 40
Bone structure, *17*
Breeding stations, 40–41

Cedro Islands, 41
Coat, 11, 24, 31, 38, 40. *See also* Molting

Dogfish, 20
Dolphins, 22

Eating habits, 20, *21*, 31, *32*, 34–37, 42
Enemies, *39*, 40
Eyes, 20

Farallon Islands, 41
Female, 18, *19*, 29–30, 31, 35, 37, *41*
Flippers, 11, 12, *13*, *17–18*, 20, *33*

Guadalupe, 40, 41

Habitat, 12, 13, 40, 41
Hauling out, 22, *23*, 24, 38

Killer whales, *39*

Male, *10*, 11–12, *14*, 15, *16*, 17, *23*, 24, *25*, 26, 27, 28–29, *30*, 36–37, 40

Manatees, 22
Mating habits, 24–30
Migration, 22, 37–38
Molting, 24, 38, 40

Pacific Ocean, 12, 40, 41
Pinniped, 15
Population, 41
Pups, 24, *31*, *32*, *33*, 34–36

Ratfish, 20, *21*, 24
Roar, 24–26

Sand flipping, *17–19*
Seals, 15
Sharks, 39
Size
    female, *16*, 17, 37
    male, 11, 12, 15, *16*, 17, 37
    pups, 31, *34*
Skates, 20, *21*
Slaughter, 38–41
    protection by law, 40
Sleeping, 22, 38
Species, 12–13
Squid, 20, *21*, 24

Teeth, 28
Trunk, *10*, 11, 15, 26–27

Walruses, 15
Weaners, 35–*36*
Whales, 22, 39
Whaling ships, 38–40